BORIS KRIGER

FREEDOM
FROM
TAXES

Introduction of Automated Payment
Transaction Tax and Universal Basic Income

What is this book about?

The world is changing at an incredible pace. Many areas do not have time to come into compliance with these changes. One of these areas is taxation and incomes.

The principle of collecting taxes from companies and individuals is flawed because it implies the possibility of tax evasion, and because high taxes really hinder the development of business and the lives of individuals, and therefore the development of the society for which these taxes are collected.

It seems worthier to blame not the system failures, but the system itself, which suggests the possibility of failures.

The principles of taxation came to us from ancient times and since then little has changed. However, it became possible to change this system, since in our time a significant part of financial transactions is carried out in electronic form, which makes it possible to automatically tax not the companies and individuals, but the movement of money itself.

The volume of financial operations is many times greater than all other economic indicators of the country, since in the financial system the same money passes from hand to hand many times. If every time they move, a small percentage is deducted to the country's budget, then this can replace all taxes, guarantee immediate replenishment of the budget, abolish the inefficient, expensive tax authorities and, most importantly, practically free the population from high taxes that currently fall intolerable mainly on the middle class.

The rich, in turn, no longer fearing persecution for tax evasion, will return capital from offshore companies (where their money often lays a dead weight) into the economies of their countries.

The poor will also replenish the budget imperceptibly for themselves, deducting a small percentage from each monetary transaction.

Such an automatic collection of taxes in the form of a low percentage of all financial transactions will strengthen the economy, prevent the deepening of economic crises, and create a system of effective fund-raising in the event of disasters and wars.

It is important that such a reform will also allow replacing the social and pension system with a universal basic income paid from the budget to the entire population of the country. And this is not a fantasy, but an absolute necessity. Computerization, robotization and automation already lead to the disappearance of many jobs. If the basic income for all is not introduced, it is fraught with insane spending on the creation of unnecessary jobs, or high unemployment, which will lead to social upheavals. It will be necessary to increase the budget of the country almost doubled in order to pay all residents the basic income, regardless of their productive work activity.

It is a tax on the total mass of financial operations that will allow for a painless for all to double the state budget, not only free people from high taxes, but also significantly improve their well-being and confidence in the future, and therefore prevent social disasters.

It is so simple and extremely beneficial to all that it is impossible to believe that such a decision would meet with resistance. Of course, the economy of the future will be based on such approaches to taxation and social security.

This book is designed to acquaint the reader with the above-mentioned ideas, thus taking a step towards a more reasonable and comfortable future for life.

Why no one likes to pay taxes?

In Gianni Rodari's children book "The Adventures of Chipollino" it is written: "Once a month, signore Tomato walked around the village houses and made the peasants breathe deeply in his presence. In turn, he measured their chest volume after inhalation and exhalation, then made a calculation and determined what amount was due from each air consumer. "

Since then, the tax system has changed little. To the one who collects the tax, in general it does not matter for what reason the tax is collected. It is important to collect a certain amount of money. So there are various excuses offered, why this money should be paid: for air and so on ... But why not do it painlessly for taxpayers and much more efficiently than it is done now? As it was once said: "One hundred thousand spectators per one dollar ... it will be ... it will be ... crazy money!" And at the same time it is not expensive for the audience.

At the moment, modern taxation looks like this: imagine a stadium for one hundred thousand spectators, then a quarter of them would pay taxes of 4 dollars each, a quarter would not pay anything at all (because it would enter the stadium without tickets). Those who try to pass free without tickets would be sluggishly and rarely caught, deprived of all property and put in jail. And a quarter of the spectators for poverty would also be paid extra dollar each, just because they came to the stadium. The organizers cannot check tickets of all. Therefore, they rely on the integrity of the audience.

But the worst thing is that the stadium owners have no guarantee that they would collect a hundred thousand dollars. Most often, they would hardly collect 75,000, and the rest they would try to extort from individual viewers who would be caught without tickets. Agree, you cannot think of a stupider and more painful system.

As the American researcher Charles Adams wrote, the similarity between tax collectors and robbers stems from the very meaning of the word "tax", which means withdrawal by force. Taxes are not debts, although we often use the expression "tax debt". In debt disputes, it is a question of returning in full the amount borrowed. There is nothing like that in tax disputes. The taxpayer owes the state simply because it is so ordered. The essence of taxes, therefore, is in the weaning of money or property by the state without direct compensation or compensation for such weaning. [1]

People at all times instinctively called tax collectors robbers because they act through threats and humiliation. The tax collector is a bureaucratic Robin Hood, who takes wealth away from everyone he gets in the way, and, like Robin Hood, the collector often does a lot of good money on the money that was taken because the state would collapse without taxes.

Taxes are the fuel that drives the locomotive of society. The most ancient civilization that we know - Sumerian, which arose six thousand years ago in Mesopotamia, - also collected taxes. There are clay tablets telling of the Sumerian city, where everything was subject to heavy taxes — the signs read: "There were tax collectors everywhere". Then came the good king, who, as stated in the tablets, "established freedom, and there were no tax collectors anywhere".

But even after six thousand years, taxes are not popular and are universally perceived as a necessary evil, with which, whether you want it or not, you have to put up with it. Moreover, such an attitude to taxes is typical both for those who carefully pay them and for those who successfully evade paying them. It is unlikely that there is at least one normal person who would get pleasure from the process of paying taxes. Not from the mantra: "pay and sleep peacefully," namely, from the very fact that he was deprived of a portion of the income.

Taxation systems are complex, cumbersome, inefficient,

costly to the state, and completely unfair. The majority of taxes are paid by the working population, the so-called middle class, which even in the most developed countries sometimes does not have enough money to maintain a decent lifestyle, and they have to go into debt.

Large corporations successfully evade taxes, using a variety of legal and not entirely legal methods.

A significant part of the population, those who work for cash — migrants and small entrepreneurs — often pay nothing to the state budget at all. Not to mention the poorest parts of the population, who are not only unable to pay taxes, but are mainly recipients of social benefits, that is, instead of replenishing the state budget, they spend it. And in general, these trends are seen in almost all countries of the world, regardless of their level of economic development.

Politicians have endless debates about how to reform taxation systems, but everything ends with half measures that do not change the essence of the problem. Disputes reach the highest level during economic crises, when the budgets of countries are experiencing particular difficulties. Some raise taxes, hoping to replenish the budget, others lower them to increase the population's motivation to pay. Some the tax structure, while the others are taken to literally "racketeer terror" of the population to extort taxes. They introduces remuneration for denunciations, to debtors they "turn on counter." But even those who are caught do not always pay. By that time, they can simply waste all their money or hide them safely. The others, feeling threatened, with even greater zeal, hide their savings in pods, take them abroad.

Such methods do not solve problems, and sometimes aggravate them. As a rule, only those who work in official jobs still pay and they don't have enough money. And they pay an exorbitant amount, from one third to one half of their earnings and even more. The rest, pretending to be law-abiding citizens, sabotage the tax system in all possible ways. Fortunately, on the one hand, there are enough ways to do this, but on the other hand, the repressive system is inefficient and, more often, it is more likely used as a lever for keeping personal or political accounts, than as a source for replenishing the treasury.

In essence, the entire population is potentially criminalized, because the charge of harboring income and tax evasion can, in principle, be presented to any individual, because the tax rules are so complex and contradictory that one way or another everyone can be guilty.

This motivates the population to cooperate with the state even less. What is the point of giving away a significant part of the hard-earned years, so that at some point, by slandering a neighbor or just by chance, would the tax leap on you and pick you up?

Many, who have at least some significant savings, try to withdraw them from the zone of jurisdiction of the countries in which they live. This is also explained by the fact that any capital attracts, like jam flies, lawsuits for various reasons, with the sole purpose of profit.

Meanwhile, the exit is very simple. It is necessary to exclude the psychological factor from the system of paying taxes, to automate taxation, making it inconspicuous and not burdensome for the population. That is, to take a little from all monetary transactions, both when multi-million transfers are made between corporation accounts, and when a student, using a credit card, buys a movie ticket on credit.

The volume of all operations is a truly astronomical amount, and the same money repeatedly passes through the system, each time allowing a small percentage to be charged to the state.

Politicians and legislators completely ignore the fact that in the modern era, an increasing amount of money passes electronically through the financial system, where it is possible to immediately and automatically impose a slight tax on any movement of money, regardless of who owns and what they are intended for deciding once and for all the problem of taxation, freeing all, including politicians themselves, from any other taxes, the need to file tax returns and the very possibility of being accused and tax evasion.

Innovations in finance, communications and transportation, capital mobility at the international level, including the presence of many offshore zones make it virtually impossible to effectively tax. But still, the laws and regulations concerning tax collection are based, as before, on the assessment of individual income, corporate income and expenses related to running a business. This leaves a lot of loopholes on both sides, both for those who are trying to reduce their taxes, and for those who are trying to counteract them.

The solution to the problem is an automatically charged tax –

The Automated Payment Transaction Tax (APT) - on cash flow.

It is a universal extremely low tax on all monetary transactions, designed to replace all other taxes and the need to file tax returns for businesses and individuals.

This approach will expand the base for tax collection. Supporters see it as a neutral income tax on transactions, the tax base of which mainly consists of financial transactions, and not personal income. It is based on the fundamental notion of taxation as "a state system through which the government receives funds to maintain financial, legal, and political institutions that protect private property rights and promote market trade and commerce." [2]

The cash flow tax extends the tax reform ideas of John Maynard Keynes [3], James Tobin [4] and Lawrence Summers [5] to their logical conclusion, namely, taxing the broadest possible tax base at the lowest possible tax rate. The goal is to significantly increase economic efficiency, increase stability in financial markets and minimize tax administration costs (assessment costs, collection, and compliance with tax rules).

This will increase the predictability of tax collection, reduce the burden of taxes on the working part of the population, which is already hard to cope with everyday difficulties, and distribute this burden on all financial transactions, making taxation completely painless and imperceptible.

Moreover, if such a tax is 0.5%, then increasing it to 1% will double the state budget. For the majority of taxpayers who are accustomed to 20-40 percent taxes, these figures do not matter, especially if we consider that the released funds can be used to introduce universal income for the entire population, replacing most of the social benefits for the poor, pension for pensioners those with higher wealth will be an additional help.

Where is usually the most money and how taxes can be collected automatically and painlessly for everyone?

Imagine Mary and Johnny. Mary has 3 apples, and Johnny 4. Their total capital is $3 + 4 = 7$ apples.

Johnny decided to let Mary hold all his apples while he was out in the washroom. And then Mary gave him all the apples, while she in turn went to powder her nose. After that, Johnny returned her 3 apples. Their total capital and its distribution remained the same. But the volume of all operations made with apples amounted to

$4 + 7 + 7 = 18$ apples

If you bite off a little bit of each apple at the time of its transfer from hand to hand, you will make 18 snacks, albeit very small, but in total it will turn out that you will eat, maybe a whole apple.

The same principle is based on the idea of a tax on all financial transactions. Only not two people participate in them, but millions of taxpayers and recipients, therefore, unlike Johnny and Mary, your snacks on their apples will be microscopic, but the result for you will be colossal.

The automatic payment transaction tax (APT tax) uses 21st century technology to automatically assess and collect taxes, while transactions are performed using electronic technology of the bank payment system. Joseph Stiglitz, former senior vice president and chief economist of the World Bank, confirmed the "technical feasibility" of collecting such a tax. Although Tobin in 1976 said that his tax idea looked impracticable, Stiglitz noted later that modern technology means that it is no longer the case, and said that collecting such a tax is "a much more accomplished task today" than several decades ago.

If you take various indicators of the country's economy, then the largest amount of money will correspond to the sum of all financial transactions taking place in its jurisdiction. After all, this amount will include the same money as they are repeatedly exchanged between payers and recipients.

To imagine the ratio of taxes collected and the total volume of financial operations in a particular country, you need to turn to examples from astronomy. In this case, the difference between them can be imagined as the difference between the size of the Sun and the Earth.

Anyone who is not familiar with astronomy can imagine a watermelon and a grape. In this case, the grape will be the sum of taxes required to fill the state budget, and the watermelon - the sum of all financial transactions.

If you simply try to estimate the volume of electronic transactions in the world, it is calculated in quadrillions of dollars a year. According to a document from the US Treasury, SWIFT processes about $ 5 trillion a day, that is, about $ 1.25 quadrillion a year. And this is only bank payments. Similarly, CHIPS processes about $ 400 trillion a year, and Fedwire processes about $ 900 trillion a year (most of them come from SWIFT messages). These transactions account for a significant proportion of electronic transactions in the world, so it is safe to assume that the total amount of transactions is several quadrillion dollars a year. It is mainly about external transfers, while within the countries these numbers will be many times more, because the same money is transferred from payers to recipients and back all the time.

The problem of taxation and crypto currency [6] of the type of bit coins is solved, since the input and output of funds when investing in crypto currency is carried out through ordinary payment tools.

Taxation of exchange transactions adds additional zeros to the enormous volume of transactions. Not to talk about such payment giants as Western Union, MoneyGram and others.

Automatic Money Movement Tax

Automatic money movement tax can replace all federal and local taxes, including income tax, value added tax, real estate taxes, inheritance taxes. This tax can be automatically collected from the accounts of taxpayers during any financial transactions. Thus, its size will be very low. And the collection of taxes will reach 100 percent efficiency and will immediately replenish the budget.

The technical support of such taxation is quite simple and does not go beyond the framework of the existing software of the modern banking system. In each financial organization a state account should be created, to which a certain percentage from all financial operations will be automatically transferred, and then the accumulated sums will be transferred to the budget with a certain periodicity.

Variable tax percentage depending on the rate of replenishment of the budget throughout the year

The percentage of tax can be variable as the established state budget is filled. That is, at the beginning of the year, this percentage will be slightly higher, and by the end of the year it may generally drop to zero. So you can solve the problem that the volume of all financial transactions is unknown in advance, and this figure can vary from year to year or during the year.

Suppose a budget is set for a certain year. At the beginning of the year, transaction tax can be set at 1%. As you fill the budget, you can reduce it to 0.5%, and by the end of the year, stop charging altogether. On the other hand, if there is a sharp decline in the volume of financial transactions, the tax can be raised to 1.5%. Thus, the replenishment of the budget will be absolutely guaranteed.

Such a low tax will not affect the behavior of the population and companies, reducing their motivation to conduct financial transactions, will not lead to an increase in cash transactions. The population and business have long been accustomed to, that banks charge them a certain fee for the commission of transactions, and often this cost is much higher than one percent.

However, if due to the introduction of tax, the volume of operations will still decrease, it will be explained to taxpayers that the more financial transactions they make, the less will be the percentage of tax during the year.

Individual tax percentage depending on the volume of financial transactions

You can put into operation a special program that would change the percentage individually for each taxpayer, depending on the volume of each operation. If there are many operations, then the tax is reduced, and if it is small, then, on the contrary, it rises.

So, for enterprises with a huge number of financial transactions, the tax will be reduced to a microscopic size.

In other words, every bank, stock brokerage office, money transfer system, such as PayPal, Yandex Money, Western Union, Money Gram, credit organizations will automatically transfer a certain percentage of all financial transactions to the state budget (according to some calculations an average of 0.35%. This applies equally to operations of multi-billion companies and buying a movie ticket, paying with a card in a store, etc.

Exemption from individual tax liability

This automatic system does not need to track who exactly the money came from, and, thus, essentially exempts individual responsibility for paying taxes.

The system completely eliminates the need to file tax returns, removes control over individual and corporate financial activities. Moreover, the state, through its tax services, will not have the need (and legal force) to stick its nose into our incomes and expenses. For the sake of this alone, it would be worthwhile to conduct such a reform everywhere.

Overcoming resistance to reform

There are practically no persons or organizations that would not like such changes in tax legislation, except for a certain number of tax officials and accountants who would lose their jobs as a result of such a reform. But they constitute an insignificant part of the population, and, in addition, it can be taken into account in legislation that all persons and organizations involved in taxation will receive significant compensation for starting a new career or business. Funds for these compensations can be taken into account in the budget and made sufficient to win over all those involved in the work with taxation.

For example, in Canada, about $ 7 billion is spent each year on the maintenance of tax services, while these services employ 40,000 people.

It turns out that in the next year after the reform, each employee can be given compensation in the amount of about $ 175,000, in the second year 50% of this amount, in the third 25%. This would help employees find new uses for their forces. The average salary of Canadian tax officials is $ 68,103 per year, which is equal to the average salary in the country, so few of them would refuse such a significant compensation. And the population would be able to get rid of these involuntary spin-grease at no additional cost, using only the funds that were already allocated for their maintenance.

Imagine an average accountant who helps people fill out tax returns. The state may, at the same time, pay to this person an amount of compensation equal to several annual incomes of this individual. In addition, there will be a need for accountants in the future - for the calculation of salaries and internal accounting of company finances.

Or imagine a tax inspector with an average salary. Even if he provides his income with some additional fraud, he will also prefer to receive a significant amount of compensation than to continue his activity. Thus, potential adversaries can be turned into ardent supporters of such a reform.

The only ones who actually start paying more taxes are large corporations that are currently actively evading taxes, but their payments on the new automatic tax would be preferable to the risks of being forced to pay real taxes in accordance with existing legislation.

The EU blamed commercial giants Amazon and Apple for not paying taxes and demanded to refund unpaid amounts to the EU budget: Amazon has to pay 250 million euros and Apple13 billion euros.

The EU Commission published a report in which it showed the economic injustice and illegality of the tax agreement concluded in Luxembourg. European Commissioner Margret Westagger said that the agreement in Luxembourg allows Amazon to pay significantly less taxes than other companies, which is illegal in accordance with EU legislation. In Luxembourg, Amazon has been granted tax breaks that allow you not to tax three-quarters of the profits. As a result, Amazon paid four times less taxes in Europe than local businesses.

The tax agreement in Luxembourg with Amazon was concluded in 2003. An investigation into the illegality of this agreement was initiated by the EU Commission in 2014. The investigation revealed that this agreement allowed Amazon EU to transfer its profits to Amazon Europe Holding Technologies, which was not taxed.

As for Apple, this technical giant received such tax breaks in Ireland that as a result paid corporate tax at a rate of no more than 1%. According to estimates of the EU Commission, Apple has not paid taxes in the amount of 13 billion euros.

But with all this, it is safe to say that such giants as Apple, Google and Amazon would agree to deduct a fraction of a percent from all transactions in return for the abolition of all taxes.

In any case, for companies that refuse to accept reform, you can leave the old way of taxation.

In general, flexibility and individualization of laws is a very promising direction. Indeed, in the end, the individual and the state are partners in a social contract and it would be more natural to negotiate with a partner than to force him to agree to the conditions dictated by the state, as is happening now.

Preventing Financial Crises

The economic crisis is characterized by a sharp and significant drop in revenues to the budget, while spending on subsidizing lagging industries and on servicing foreign debt is increasing. Thus, there is a snowball, some noose. The stronger the crisis, the less money is in the budget and fewer opportunities are there for the state to rectify the situation. An increase in taxes leads to a further reduction in production, to tax evasion, and in the end it only worsens the situation.

With the introduction of a variable automatic tax on all financial transactions replenishment of the budget will be guaranteed. Reducing the volume of transactions will not lead to a budget deficit due to a slight increase in the percentage of automatic tax. In turn, such a change in tax will not have a negative impact on the economy.

Thus, the automatic tax on all financial transactions can serve as a brake on the deepening of the economic crisis, and, moreover, reverse it due to the possibility of supporting lagging industries from the replenished budget.

Budget Growth Restriction

Another danger is bloating the budget. Parliamentarians (dreamers at the expense of the people) could inflate the budget so that a small tax on all transactions becomes significant. Therefore, it is necessary by law, perhaps even constitutionally, to limit the increase in the budget, making it dependent not on the success of the economy, but on the volume of cash transactions. For example, if last year the required amount to replenish the budget could be collected in accordance with the following percentage change:

Winter   Spring Summer Autumn

0.45% 0.35% 0.25% 0.15%

you can leave the percentage of tax for autumn 0.25% and transfer additional funds to the budget of the next year

Thus, if the budget for 2025 would be 100 billion and this amount would already be collected by the end of the summer, then in the fall an additional 5 billion would be collected into the budget of next year, which could be increased to 105 billion. Thus, an increase in the budget would occur not at the expense of the expected revenues for the next year, but on the basis of the collected additional revenues for the previous one. Of course, computer simulations would be required to derive the most optimal formulas for calculating the variable tax on financial transactions.

Reduction of external debt

At present, when the state does not have enough money, but for some reason it cannot increase tax collection, the state launches a printing press and increases the issue of money (now, instead of typing, it's enough to add zeros in the computer - saving on paper and paint) .

The emission will lead to inflation, the depreciation of the national currency and other negative consequences.

Another way - loans, internal and external. But with the deterioration of the economy, voluntary loans provided by domestic loans have little hope and, thus, the external debt increases with an increase in the cost of its servicing. In extreme cases, the situation leads to a default, which arises when the sovereign state is unable to pay the debt. A sovereign state, by definition, cannot be forced to pay its debts [7]. However, it can face significant pressure. Today Article 2 of the UN Charter prohibits the use of force in such cases, but in the past this has happened more than once [8]. Anyway, a default can lead to a full or partial loss of independence of the country or its economic isolation.

Automatic tax on financial transactions would allow to solve this problem without serious consequences for the economy and the population. It is enough to increase the percentage of this tax by one tenth, and the budget would receive funds comparable to multi-billion loans. The fact is that the population and business cannot live without everyday financial transactions. And, no matter how bad the economic situation of the country, these operations would still be carried out. An increase in the percentage charged from all operations would fill the budget.

Crisis situations

If we introduce a law on crisis situations (war, natural disasters, epidemics), then it would allow for a limited time to raise the tax to the required value. It is also necessary to establish strict supervision over the validity of such decisions and the use of funds. Thus, the state would become much more stable in case of any crises.

Tax collection costs reduction

In the United States in 2018, nearly $ 11 billion was requested for the maintenance of tax services. [9] Interestingly, in Canada, in a country with a population 10 times smaller than in the US, as already mentioned, $ 7.8 billion was spent on the maintenance of the tax service in 2014.

Of course, with respect to the taxes collected, this amount is probably insignificant, but in its absolute value it is quite high and it can be used better.

CRITICISM OF THE EXISTING SYSTEM OF TAXATION

The subject of taxation is relevant, since any state with the help of taxes has an impact on the economic system of the country.

Taxes simultaneously perform four main functions: fiscal, distributive, regulatory and controlling. [10]

The fiscal function of taxation is the main function of taxation. Historically, it is the most ancient and at the same time, the main: taxes are a predominant component of the state budget revenues. The implementation of this function is carried out at the expense of tax control and tax sanctions, which ensure maximum collection of established taxes and create obstacles to tax evasion. Simply put, this is a collection of taxes in favor of the state. Thanks to this function, the main purpose of taxes is realized: the formation and mobilization of financial resources of the state. All other functions of taxation are derived from the fiscal. In any case, along with purely financial and fiscal objectives, taxes may pursue the others, for example, economic or social ones. In other words, financial goals, being the most significant, are not exceptional. Automatic tax on financial transactions will effectively and fully perform the fiscal function of taxation and will eliminate the system of control and repression.

The fact is that for its implementation, on the one hand, neither consent nor any taxpayer's assistance is required, on the other hand, it is almost unlikely and impossible to counteract on his part.

The distribution (social) function of taxation consists in the redistribution of social income (the transfer of funds in favor of the weaker and more unprotected categories of citizens occurs by imposing a tax burden on stronger categories of the population). It must be said that such redistribution guarantees social peace and reduces the likelihood of revolutionary upheavals. Usually, the state does not cope well with this function due to the constant lack of budget. Automatic tax on financial transactions will effectively replenish and increase the budget. Thus, there will be enough funds to introduce universal income for the entire population. Pensions, social benefits will no longer be needed. All, regardless of any conditions, will receive a certain monthly income.

The regulatory function of taxation is aimed at solving through tax mechanisms of various tasks of the state economic policy. According to the eminent English economist John Keynes, taxes exist in society exclusively to regulate economic relations. In the framework of the regulatory function of taxation, there are three subfunctions: stimulating, discouraging and reproduction.

The stimulating sub-function of taxation is aimed at supporting the development of certain economic processes. It is implemented through a system of benefits and exemptions. The current tax system provides a wide range of tax benefits to small businesses, enterprises of the disabled, agricultural producers, organizations that make capital investments in production and charitable activities, etc.

The disincentive sub-function of taxation is aimed at imposing, through the tax burden, obstacles to the development of any economic processes.

Reproductive subfunction is intended for the accumulation of funds for the restoration of used resources. This subfunction is performed by deductions for the reproduction of the mineral resource base, water charges, etc.

The introduction of automatic income for all financial transactions would allow the state to more effectively carry out the regulatory function primarily by the fact that the state, in general, would not care from which sources the money comes to the budget.

In the course of the implementation of tax laws, many acute problems arise concerning the relationship between taxpayers and the state, the responsibility of individuals and legal entities for the implementation of tax legislation, the rights and obligations of tax authorities. In order to determine ways of reforming the tax system, it is necessary, first of all, to analyze the main problems of the tax system and fees of the country at the present stage of civilization development. Among these problems are the following [11]:

1. The diseconomy and inefficiency of the tax system to meet the challenges of collecting tax payments and budgeting;

2. A significant number of various taxes, high tax rates, which greatly contributes to tax evasion by taxpayers;

3. Ineffective, humiliating and fundamentally unfair system of criminal prosecution for tax evasion.

4. The entanglement of legislation. A large number of

legislation, a huge number of benefits and rules makes the tax system complex and controversial;

5. Underestimation or reassessment of the role and value of certain types of taxes contributes to frequent changes in tax legislation, tax base, tax rates, and other changes in tax acts, which does not make the tax system stable;

Automatic tax on financial transactions wouldll allow to effectively and completely solve these problems.

EXCLUSION OF POSSIBILITY OF TAX EVASION

Tax evasion is carried out by individuals, corporations and trusts. Taxpayers sometimes do not file tax returns at all, do business through companies open to other people, deliberately distort the actual state of their affairs in tax authorities to reduce their tax liabilities, produce fictitious tax reporting, for example, declaring smaller incomes than actually earned amounts, or overpricing.

One measure of the degree of tax evasion is the amount of unregistered income, which is the difference between the amount of income that must be reported to the tax authorities and the actual amount reported in the financial declaration.

But the fact is that the tax authorities do not even suspect the majority of hidden incomes, so it is impossible to realistically estimate the amount of uncollected taxes. In addition, too large numbers may cause the public to doubt the efficiency of the tax authorities, which, of course, is not profitable for them. Therefore, it can be assumed that the true amount of under-collecting taxes can be much higher than those used by official statistics.

For example, take the law-abiding Canada, assuming that in other countries the situation with tax collection can be much worse.

According to the Toronto Star newspaper, the federal government recognizes that annually unpaid taxes amount to $ 47.8 billion. [12]

These billions represent only a fraction of all taxes that remain unpaid, as they do not include taxes owed to the provinces and municipalities — all of which need additional revenues to cover the budget deficit and the implementation of large public works projects.

Active tax evasion, as well as errors in filing tax returns and failure to pay taxes, complete the causes of the loss of tax revenues.

Despite a promise during the last election campaign, Ottawa did not provide the official tax deficit figure — an estimate of the difference between all taxes payable on paper and actual tax revenues collected by the government.

Indeed, the average entrepreneur can make money well without paying a penny of taxes, and most often he will not be punished. Yes, even if the punishment would be inevitable, people would continue to find loopholes. And in existing conditions, special ingenuity is not required.

The fact is that even if the tax service makes a complaint to an entrepreneur, it will happen not earlier than one and a half, or even two or three years after the actual receipt of money for which the tax was not paid. By that time, most of the money was gone.

DECRIMINALIZATION OF POPULATION

The potential threat of criminal prosecution for tax evasion demoralizes and criminalizes society. Everyone sees in the state an enemy who can deprive of freedom and accumulated funds.

The psychology of a citizen, forming in such conditions, easily allows to go to other financial crimes, forgery, and even fraud, because if the threat of persecution exists, then what is there to fear ...

Political and financial figures, vulnerable from the point of view of tax disclosures, for the most part are forced to live a double life and are easily manipulated through checking their tax returns.

The publication of secret offshore accounts in recent years has caused a series of high-profile resignations. Why is all this necessary? To keep people in check ... There is no other explanation. After all, a universal tax on money would make such a situation impossible.

CANCELLATION OF CASH

In developed countries, the issue of withdrawing physical cash and replacing them with electronic money has already been practically resolved. In the United States and Europe, only 5 to 10 percent of the population continues to use cash. Even without any reforms, cash will soon disappear through natural "extinction". Moreover, the introduction of a tax on the movement of money and the abolition of the need to declare income will lead to the disappearance of the last incentives to withdraw funds in cash.

Only the criminal realm remains. But here, oddly enough, anonymous means of electronic payments should be introduced, and then the state will replenish the budget from criminal financial transactions. Depriving the criminal world of cash settlement will in no way stop criminal activity. Therefore, it is perfectly acceptable to allow any citizen to make payments anonymously, not only without taking into account his potentially criminal intentions, but simply because of the protection of his personal data. For example, if he does not want to advertise the purchase of Viagra or alcohol. Such anonymous means of payment already exist in the form of special cards. If there is no need for the state to extort taxes from the population, then there is no need to keep track of who, how and how much spends his money.

RETURN OF OFFSHORE CAPITALS

The return of offshore capital would lead to a significant economic recovery.

According to the US Department of Commerce, which Bloomberg refers to, corporations returned $ 664.9 billion to the United States in 2018, which is significantly higher than in 2017, when funds in the amount of $ 155.1 billion were returned.

Nevertheless, Donald Trump stated that the companies "will soon return more than $ 4 trillion" due to the reduction of taxes taken by his administration in 2017. In his speech at a meeting with heads of companies in August 2018, he announced the return of "$ 4–5 trillion" to the United States.

You can imagine how much money is actually in offshore ...

UNIVERSAL GUARANTEED BASIC INCOME
We all learned in the history lessons in school the chapters on "engine destroyers," the so-called Luddites. These are

participants in the spontaneous protests of the first quarter of the XIX century against the introduction of cars during the industrial revolution in England. From the point of view of the Luddites, engines forced people out of the production, which led to technological unemployment. Often the protest was expressed in pogroms and the destruction of machinery and equipment.

Now the process of crowding people out of their jobs is taking on a grand scale. The introduction of the use of automatic passenger and freight cars will lead to the fact that many thousands of drivers will be out of work. The introduction of effective Internet education will replace thousands of teachers, automatic tellers are already replacing people. This process goes on in almost all spheres of human activity. It is especially extensive and imperceptible in production, where already entire plants switch to automatic mode.

Massive job losses can lead to social upheaval.

Therefore, the state still ignores the automation process and sometimes creates unnecessary jobs for anyone to improve accountability and reduce unemployment. In this case, funds from taxes are wasted. To create a workplace, you need a lot more money than just paying a worker a benefit in the amount of his salary.

But the moment will come when the automation process will become so powerful that nothing can plug the holes. Mass unemployment is inevitable. Therefore, oddly enough, instead of keeping up with progress, this remarkable process is hampered by the creation of artificially needed jobs.

The process of replacing people with robots and computers, creating artificial intelligence is also hampered by the fact that people – workers and society as a whole – are conservative. Employers do not trust engines and continue to prefer to hire people. Buyers in stores also communicate more likely with live sellers than with automatic cash registers. This is due to the imperfections of the latter.

But if people are given an unconditional (guaranteed) basic income, then a certain part of them will give up on low-paying boring jobs and thereby create a shortage in the labor market, and this, in turn, will push the process of robotization.

People can also be offered to do self-development and volunteering. And for those who lack basic income, continue to work in areas where robotization is not yet possible.

In addition, the sharp introduction of universal income can lead to a collapse of the labor market, even if many claim that they will continue to work anyway. The economy is not yet ready for this, and therefore it is necessary to introduce basic income gradually, in the form of annually increasing surcharges to existing income.

Unconditional (guaranteed) basic income [13] (unconditional basic income of AML) is a social concept, which involves the regular payment of a certain amount of money to each member of society by the state. Payments are made to all residents, regardless of income level and without the need to perform work.

The experiment on the introduction of unconditional basic income from January 1, 2017 to 2019 took place in Finland, a similar experiment took place in Canada and in many other countries.

The first pan-European survey in April 2016 showed that 64% of the inhabitants of the European Union would support the introduction of unconditional basic income. 35% are aware of AML, 23% say they fully understand the essence and objectives of this program, a quarter have heard of it, 17% know nothing about AML. It should be emphasized that only 4% of citizens after the introduction of AML will refuse to work. People consider the most convincing advantages of AML to be that such social payments "reduce anxiety about basic financial needs" (40%) [14] and help to ensure equal opportunities for people (31%) [15].

The introduction of unconditional basic income can provide a decent standard of living, free up time for creativity and education, overcome the consequences of the massive loss of jobs due to the development of robotics and become an alternative to the state social security system [16].

Currently, in different countries, politicians, economists and sociologists are discussing the possibility of different models of a guaranteed minimum.

Suzanne Vist, for example, offers an automatic monthly increase in the bank account of every German citizen by 1,500 (one thousand five hundred) euros - for each adult and 1,000 (thousand) euros - for each child [17].

Prof. Franz Hörmann, a professor at the University of Economics in Vienna [de], considers that an unconditional income is also necessary in the form of a minimum set of goods and services [18].

 Basic income would show the world real democratic freedom, the right to a decent life, the right to freedom from slave labor, solve the problem of poverty and the problem of technological unemployment. Reduce the problem of economic inequality. Reduce crime rates.

Reduce health care costs, because people will have more opportunities to monitor their health. Many works, alas, do not contribute to a healthy lifestyle, and some are directly detrimental to health.

Basic income will reduce the cost of administering social programs, since it does not require checking for compliance with the criteria for providing assistance. This is a much simpler and more transparent social security system than the one that exists today in social states around the world. Instead of having numerous social security programs, there will simply be a universal unconditional income. Estimating the required funds or similar administrative measures would save money on social security that could be spent on grants. The Basic Income Network (BIN) describes one of the advantages of basic income as a lower total cost than current expenditure on social benefits [19].

Such an income will allow people to do what they want, not what the market requires.

Basic income can reduce poverty or even eradicate poverty. The ability of basic income to eradicate poverty is indisputable, since by definition it is true that unconditional income set above the poverty line will eliminate poverty. It is somewhat controversial whether this level of basic income is sustainable. But basic income can be monthly indexed according to certain indicators, such as the consumer basket.

Basic income potentially contributes to economic growth: people can decide to invest in themselves in order to earn more, get interesting and well-paid jobs, which, in turn, can trigger growth.

Unconditional basic income exempts people in free social

security from the paternalistic oversight of conditional social security policies, which reduce people's motivation to actively and openly earn money for fear of losing social benefits and benefits.

The basic income is needed to protect against the arbitrariness of the authorities in order to be able to say no. The fact is that if any other group of people controls the resources necessary for survival, the person does not have a reasonable choice but to do what the group controlling the resources requires. Prior to the creation of governments and landlords, people had direct access to the resources necessary for survival. But today, the resources needed for food, shelter and clothing are privatized in such a way that some get a share, while others do not. From this point of view, the basic income weakens the link between survival and the restriction of pluralism, provides economic freedom, which, combined with political freedom, religious freedom and personal freedom, establishes the status of each person as a free individual [20].

What are the arguments against the introduction of basic income? Criticism of the concept of unconditional basic income is based on economic and legal arguments.

It is believed that the system will require large expenditures. This is true. If the volume of all financial transactions is difficult to determine, then calculating how much money is required for basic income is quite simple. It is necessary to multiply the population of the country by the annual basic income.

For example, for Canada, this figure is calculated as follows. The population is 37 million. If we take the sum of $ 2,000 per month for basic income, then we need $ 24,000 per inhabitant per country per year.

Multiply 37 million by 24 thousand and get 888 billion. Currently, the Canadian federal budget, together with the provincial budgets, is about the same amount. [21]

Consequently, if you double the budget by half, you can pay each resident of the country $ 2,000 per month. Where to get this money? The problem is solved by a universal tax on the movement of money. That is, if it is 1 percent, then it is necessary that 170 trillion dollars a year pass through the financial system of Canada. It is rather difficult to count how many actually pass through the country's financial systems. But if we take into account that the same money in the system is circulated many times, it can be assumed that this amount is not less than 170 trillion. However, it is not necessary to calculate this amount exactly. It is enough to introduce a flexible tax and adjust it depending on the amount collected.

The main thing is the principle. Even if we are mistaken 10 times (which is very unlikely), and the tax will have to be levied at a rate of 10 percent, anyway, the positive effect of such a reform will be enormous.

And finally, another argument against. What will people do if they are given enough money for nothing? Will this not lead to personal degradation? Drug addiction? Dependence on computer games? Such naive questions could be possible already in the XIX century. If you reduce the working day from 16 to 12 hours, would not people get drunk in the vacant time? That could be. But if you do not develop the promotion of a creative approach to life, do not provide people with positive alternatives to slave labor either.

There is also the danger that universal income, by increasing consumption, will lead to even greater depletion of resources. An approach to solving this problem is given in the next chapter.

ALTERNATIVE TO THE SOCIETY OF CONSUMPTION

For the development of the economy it doesn't matter how you spend your money. The main thing is that you spend it. Money is blood in the circulatory system of society, and blood must move like in a living organism. Otherwise - death.

That is why the consumer society constantly increases our needs, offering all new products and services, forcing to throw out almost new things, replacing them with others. If only there was a movement of money.

But the fact is that money can be spent on things that do not reduce our natural resources and do not stimulate a system of meaningless consumption. It is about acquiring knowledge with the help of training programs, art, literature, and the help of one's neighbor through charity. The whole point is that people do not hide money in bank accounts, because if there is no movement of money, then it is impossible to collect a universal tax on financial transactions.

Thus, a concept appeared with an unfortunate name, but a very good meaning.

Anti-growth (Fr. décroissance; the English degrowth) - a socio-economic concept, stating the need to reduce the size of the economy to ensure social welfare in the long term. In contrast to the growth-oriented economy, anti-growth implies targeted economic and social transformation [22] with the aim of maximizing the level of happiness and well-being due to the fact that the time freed from the reduction of personal consumption and the effective organization of social labor is devoted to arts, family, culture and community. The concept of anti-growth was formulated in the 1970s after the publication of the report of the Rome Club "The Limits to Growth" and the publication of the work of Nicholas Georgescu-Regen "The Law of Entropy and the Economic Process". [23].

Anti-growth criticizes the fixation of the modern world on consumption. Consumerism, as a rule, becomes possible due to inequality, leads to environmental degradation, and also does not provide a meaningful and happy life. The time available for reducing personal consumption and effectively organizing basic income can be devoted to the arts, music, family, culture and society.

But it does not necessarily reduce the volume of the economy. It is just necessary to redirect it from material consumption, harming the environment, to the consumption of spiritual values.

How to improve the welfare of society by abolishing ordinary taxes and introducing basic income for all

The world has changed. Unprecedented progress is observed in how we use communication and automation. Unnoticed by us, many industries and production abandon human labor and move to partial or even complete robotization. However, taxation and welfare of the population remained almost at the level of two hundred years ago.

The principle of collecting taxes from companies and individuals is flawed because it implies the possibility of tax evasion, moreover, the true extent of tax evasion is unknown and may be an order of magnitude larger than the estimates of tax authorities. Tax collection is unfair and uneven. This system is highly adventurous and lightly controlled and, in fact, resembles robbery on a high road. "Who got caught - hold on. The rest can breathe easy"...

High taxes really hinder the development of business and the lives of individuals, lead to the impoverishment of the middle class, and therefore hinder the development of the society for which these taxes are supposed to be collected. Sometimes tax authorities simply destroy businesses and companies!

As already noted, the blame is not on system failures, but on the system itself, which suggests the possibility of failures.

Nowadays, it has become possible to change this system, since a significant part of financial transactions is carried out in electronic form, which allows you to automatically tax not the companies and individuals, but the movement of money itself.

The volume of financial operations is many times greater than all other economic indicators of the country, since in the financial system the same money passes from hand to hand many times. If each time they move deduct of a small percentage into the country's budget, this can replace all taxes, guarantee immediate replenishment of the budget, abolish the inefficient, expensive tax authorities and, most importantly, practically free the population from high taxes that currently bear an unbearable burden on the middle class.

Such a reform will also allow replacing the social and pension system with a universal basic income paid from the budget to the entire population of the country. And this is not a fantasy, but an absolute necessity. Computerization, robotization and automation already lead to the disappearance of many jobs. If the basic income for all is not introduced, it is fraught with insane spending on the creation of unnecessary jobs, or high unemployment, which will lead to social upheavals.

It is a tax on the total mass of financial operations that will allow for a painless for all to double the state budget, not only free people from high taxes, but also significantly improve their well-being and confidence in the future, and therefore prevent social disasters.

It is so simple and extremely beneficial to all that it is impossible to believe that such a decision would meet with resistance. Of course, the economy of the future will be based on such approaches to taxation and social security.

The reforms described in this book can become useless if the state continues to waste budget funds on meaningless projects, sometimes beneficial to one of the stakeholders, and sometimes simply being implemented for some political purposes.

Direct democracy, based on frequent electronic referendums, the adoption of laws and budgets based on direct electronic voting, up to the abolition of parliaments in the form in which they exist today, should prevent senseless spending, allocation of aid to warring states and other nonsense and direct electoral fraud, which modern politics is full of.

If the state is not put under the real control of its citizens, then no reforms will lead to a better life, and in the end will be again distorted beyond recognition and turned into a new noose for the population.

[1] C. Adams. For Good and Evil: the impact of taxes on the world civilization. – Lanham, Md. Madison Books, 2001.

[2] Rethinking Taxation: The Automated Payment Transaction (APT) tax By Edgar L. Feige, professor-emeritus of economics at the University of Wisconsin (Madison)

[3] Keynes, J.M. (1936). The General Theory of Employment, Interest and Money, Harcourt Brace, New York, NY.

[4] Tobin, James (July 1978). "A proposal for international monetary reform". Eastern Economic Journal. 4 (3–4): 153–159.

[5] Summers,, Lawrence; Summers, V. P. (1989). "When Financial Markets Work Too Well : A Cautious Case For A Securities Transactions Tax". Journal of Financial Services Research. 3 (2–3)

[6] A. Rosic. What is Cryptocurrency: 21-century Unicorn or the Money of the Future? - https://blockgeeks.com/guides/what-is-cryptocurrency/.

[7] Borensztein, E. The Costs of Sovereign Default: Theory and Reality. VOXLACEA (Nov 10, 2010).

[8] Reinhart, Carmen M. This time is different: Eight Centuries of Financial Folly (p. 54ff) / Carmen M. Reinhart, Kenneth S. Rogoff. — Princeton University Press, 2009. — ISBN 0-691-14216-5.

[9] Internal Revenue Service – Treasury.gov

[10] J. Kagan. Taxes Definition. - https://www.investopedia.com/terms/t/taxes.asp.

[11] R. M. Sommerfeld. Tax Reform and the Alliance for Progress. –

www.books.google.ca/books?id=_cvvDQAAQBAJ&p.

[12] «Canada misses out on nearly $50 billion in tax each year.» Toronto Star. Mon., Feb. 13, 2017

[13] A. Beckett. Post-work: the radical idea of a world without jobs. // The Gardian. - https://www.theguardian.com/news/2018/jan/19/post-work-the-radical-idea-of-a-world-without-jobs.

[14] Chohan, Usman W. Universal Basic Income: A Review (англ.) // Social Science Research Network (SSRN). — 2017. — 4 August. — DOI:10.2139/ssrn.3013634.

[15] Nico Jaspers. What do Europeans think about basic income? (англ.). BIEN (April 2016). Дата обращения 16 января 2018.

[16] Are We Approaching a Post-Work Economy? - https://www.persado.com/2016/05/post-work-economy.

[17] GrundeinkommenImBundestag.blogspot.com

[18] Daniela Rom. "Banken erfinden Geld aus Luft". derStandard.at (13. Oktober 2010).

[19] Guy, Standing. How Cash Transfers Promote the Case for Basic Income (англ.) // Basic Income Studies. — 2008. — 11 July (vol. 3, iss. 1). — ISSN 1932-0183.

[20] Philippe Van Parijs. A Basic Income for All (англ.). Boston Review (October 2000).

[21] Annual Financial Report of the Government of Canada Fiscal Year 2017–2018

[22] Demaria, F., F. Schneider, F. Sekulova and J. Martinez-Alier (2013) 'What is degrowth? From an activist slogan to a social movement .', Environmental Values, 22(2): 191-215.

[23] The Limits to Growth. -

http://www.donellameadows.org/wp-content/userfiles/Limits-to-Growth-digital-scan-version.pdf; N. Georgescu-Roegen. The Entropy Law and the Economic Process. - http://college.holycross.edu/eej/Volume12/V12N1P3_25.pdf.

www.ingramcontent.com/pod-product-compliance
Lightning Source LLC
Chambersburg PA
CBHW050351290526
45785CB00006B/2732